18.95

SUPER GROSS CREEPY-CRAWLY PROJECTS

Elsie Olson

Consulting Editor, Diane Craig, M.A./Reading Specialist

Super Sandcastle

An Imprint of Abdo Publishing
abdobooks.com

ABDOBOOKS.COM

Published by Abdo Publishing, a division of ABDO, PO Box 398166, Minneapolis, Minnesota 55439. Copyright © 2019 by Abdo Consulting Group, Inc. International copyrights reserved in all countries. No part of this book may be reproduced in any form without written permission from the publisher. Super SandCastle™ is a trademark and logo of Abdo Publishing.

Printed in the United States of America, North Mankato, Minnesota

102018
012019

THIS BOOK CONTAINS RECYCLED MATERIALS

Design and Production: Mighty Media, Inc.
Editor: Megan Borgert-Spaniol
Cover Photographs: Mighty Media, Inc.; Shutterstock
Interior Photographs: iStockphoto; Mighty Media, Inc.; Shutterstock

The following manufacturers/names appearing in this book are trademarks: Anchor®, CVSHealth®, Elmer's®, Hershey's®, Jell-O®, Knox®, Land O'Lakes®, Market Pantry™, Pyrex®

Library of Congress Control Number: 2018948862

Publisher's Cataloging-in-Publication Data
Names: Olson, Elsie, author.
Title: Super gross creepy-crawly projects / by Elsie Olson.
Description: Minneapolis, Minnesota : Abdo Publishing, 2019 | Series: Super simple super gross science
Identifiers: ISBN 9781532117305 (lib. bdg.) | ISBN 9781532170164 (ebook)
Subjects: LCSH: Insects--Juvenile literature. | Bugs--Juvenile literature. | Science--Experiments--Juvenile literature. | Science--Methodology--Juvenile literature.
Classification: DDC 507.8--dc23

Super SandCastle™ books are created by a team of professional educators, reading specialists, and content developers around five essential components—phonemic awareness, phonics, vocabulary, text comprehension, and fluency—to assist young readers as they develop reading skills and strategies and increase their general knowledge. All books are written, reviewed, and leveled for guided reading and early reading intervention programs for use in shared, guided, and independent reading and writing activities to support a balanced approach to literacy instruction.

TO ADULT HELPERS

The projects in this title are fun and simple. There are just a few things to remember to keep kids safe. Some projects require the use of sharp or hot objects. Also, kids may be using messy materials such as glue or paint. Make sure they protect their clothes and work surfaces. Review the projects before starting, and be ready to assist when necessary.

KEY SYMBOLS

Watch for these warning symbols in this book. Here is what they mean.

HOT!
You will be working with something hot. Get help!

SHARP!
You will be working with a sharp object. Get help!

CONTENTS

SUPER GROSS!

There are tons of super gross things in the world. These things can make you feel **disgust**. But did you know this feeling can keep you safe? It stops you from touching or eating things that might be harmful.

Disgusting things can still be fun to think about. That's why many people are **fascinated** by gross things. And creepy-crawly critters can be especially gross!

CREEPY-CRAWLY CRITTERS

Creepy-crawly critters come in all forms. Some, like spiders and centipedes, have many legs. Others, like worms and snakes, have no legs. These creepy critters scurry and slither all around us. They can be pretty gross. But they are very important creatures!

ALL ABOUT CREEPY-CRAWLY CRITTERS

Creepy-crawly animals may seem **disgusting**, but they are important parts of their **ecosystems**!

SPIDERS

Most spiders eat insects. They help keep insect populations from getting too high. They also eat insects that carry **diseases** that can make humans sick!

SNAKES

Most snakes eat insects and other small animals. But the biggest snakes can eat larger animals, including jaguars! Snakes help control prey populations in their **ecosystems**.

MAGGOTS

Maggots are the wormlike larvae of flies and other insects. Maggots eat dead plant and animal matter. Some hospitals even use maggots to remove dead matter from human wounds. This prevents **infection**!

MATERIALS

WIRE

CHENILLE STEMS

HEAVY CREAM

SMALL ROCKS

CLAY

HOT GLUE GUN

POPCORN KERNELS

BRASS FASTENERS

STRAWS

TOY BUGS

DENTAL FLOSS

WORMS

BANANA PUDDING

BLACK CRAFT FOAM

COCOA POWDER

CREAM OF TARTAR

TISSUE PAPER

UNFLAVORED GELATIN POWDER

BLACK POM-POMS

DUCT TAPE

9

CHOCOLATE BUG PRINTS

These creepy bug prints smell sweet!

MATERIALS

- measuring cups and spoons
- flour
- salt
- cocoa powder
- cream of tartar
- large bowl
- spoon
- vegetable oil
- vanilla
- water
- baking sheet
- plate
- toy bugs

1 Stir together 2 cups of flour, ½ cup of salt, ½ cup of cocoa powder, and 1 tablespoon of cream of tartar in a large bowl.

2 Add 3 tablespoons of vegetable oil and ½ teaspoon of vanilla to the bowl.

3 With an adult's help, add 1½ cups of boiling water to the bowl. Stir the mixture until it forms a thick dough.

4 Place the dough on a baking sheet and knead it with your hands.

5 Move the dough to a plate and press it into a flat circle.

6 Press the bugs into the dough to make creepy critter prints!

11

SPOOKY SPIDERWEB

Weave your own spiderweb in any pattern you choose!

MATERIALS

- black craft foam
- cardboard
- scissors
- pushpins
- clay
- dental floss
- materials for crafting a spider

1   Cut the craft foam and cardboard into rectangles of the same size. Lay the craft foam on top of the cardboard. Put a pushpin through each corner of the foam to secure it to the cardboard.

2   On the cardboard side, push a small ball of clay over the point of each pushpin.

3   Push more pushpins into the craft foam. Scatter the pins however you'd like.

4   Tie the end of the dental floss around one push pin.

5   Weave the floss around the pins to make a web. When you are finished, cut the floss, and tie the loose end around a pushpin.

6   Make and decorate your own spider. Then place the spider on its web!

13

EDIBLE MAGGOTS

These baby flies are squishy and gross, but they taste sweet!

MATERIALS 🔥

- straws
- scissors
- small paper cup
- 3.4-ounce box of banana pudding mix
- 2 packets of unflavored gelatin powder
- large bowl
- water
- measuring cups
- heavy cream
- spoon
- small container
- plate

1 Cut the straws into 2-inch (5 cm) pieces. Then tightly pack the pieces into a cup.

2 Pour the pudding and gelatin mixtures into a large bowl. With an adult's help, add 3 cups of boiling water to the bowl.

3 Add ¾ cup of heavy cream to the bowl. Stir the mixture, then let it cool for a few minutes.

4 Put the cup of straws into a container to catch spills. Pour the mixture into the cup so it fills the straws. Then refrigerate the cup until the mixture is firm.

5 Cut and peel down a side of the cup. Take a straw from the bunch and hold it over a plate. Gently squeeze the straw from one end until a maggot slips out. Repeat to make a plate of **edible** maggots!

VENUS FLYTRAP CATCH

Make a fun game based on a bug-eating plant!

MATERIALS

- 2 paper plates
- green and pink paint
- paintbrushes
- scissors
- chenille stems
- duct tape
- stapler
- waxed paper
- glue
- black pom-poms
- gems

1 Paint the bottom of one paper plate green. Paint the top of the other plate pink. Let the plates dry.

2 Cut the chenille stems into pieces that are each about 3 inches (7.6 cm) long.

3 Turn the pink plate upside down. Tape the chenille stem pieces around the outside edge of the plate.

4 Fold the pink paper plate in half so the pink sides face each other.

5 Cut the green paper plate in half.

Continued on the next page.

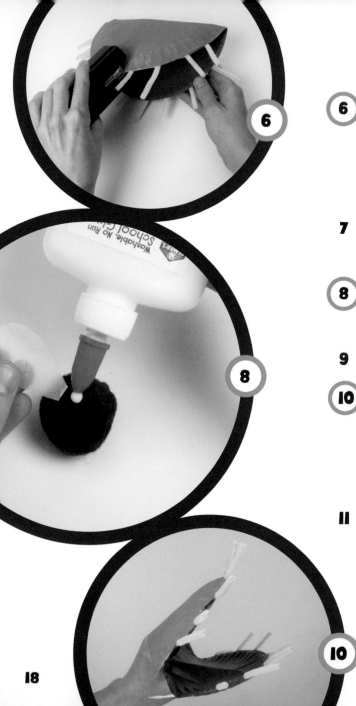

6. Line up one plate half with one side of the folded plate so the unpainted sides face each other. Staple the two plates together around the curved edges.

7. Flip the folded plate over and repeat step 6 with the other plate half.

8. To make the flies, cut wings out of waxed paper and glue them to the pom-poms.

9. Glue gems onto the pom-poms for eyes.

10. It's time to play! Hold onto the folded plate so you are wearing the Venus flytrap like a baseball glove. You should be able to open and close the Venus flytrap with your hand.

11. Have a friend toss the flies toward you. Can you catch them with your bug-eating plant?

Grossed Out!

The Venus flytrap is an excellent hunter. Its leaves are covered with tiny hairs. When an insect touches the hairs, the plant snaps shut, trapping the insect inside. Then, **digestive** juices break down the insect over several days!

COCKROACH RACER

This creepy car looks like a cockroach scurrying from a dark corner!

MATERIALS

- scissors
- straw
- wire
- 4 buttons of equal size
- small clothespin
- hot glue gun
- plastic spoon
- tissue paper
- glue stick
- chenille stem

1. Cut two 1-inch (2.5 cm) pieces of straw. Cut two 4-inch (10 cm) pieces of wire.

2. Thread the ends of one wire piece through two holes of a button. Then push the wire ends into one end of a straw piece and out the other end.

3. Thread the wire ends from step 2 through two holes of a second button. Twist the ends together. Turn the buttons to make sure the wire can move within the straw. This makes one wheel and **axle** set.

4. Repeat steps 2 and 3 to make another wheel and axle set.

Continued on the next page.

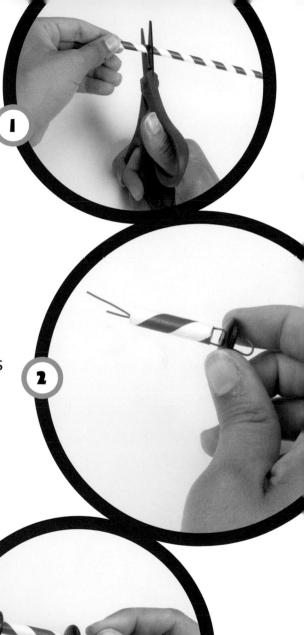

5 Hot glue the center of one **axle** to the inside of the clothespin's jaws.

6 Glue the second axle to the inside of the clothespin's handle.

7 Carefully break the handle off a plastic spoon. The spoon bowl represents the shell of the cockroach.

8 Cut wings out of tissue paper and attach them to the spoon with a glue stick.

9. Cut chenille stems to make antennae and hot glue them to one end of the spoon.

10. Hot glue the spoon to the clothespin. Push your cockroach around to creep out your family and friends!

Grossed Out!

Did you know a cockroach can live for up to a week without its head? Cockroaches are resilient creatures. They have been on Earth since the dinosaurs lived! But these creepy-crawly critters can spread many diseases. That's why to humans, cockroaches are unwelcome pests!

WORMS AT WORK

Build a cozy home for some wriggly worms.

MATERIALS ✎

- large clear plastic bottle
- scissors
- hole punch
- small rocks
- spoon
- sand
- dirt
- worms
- worm food, such as fruit and vegetable peels
- water
- duct tape
- dark construction paper
- markers
- clear tape

1 With an adult's help, carefully cut the top off the bottle at the point where it starts to curve in.

2 Use a hole punch to poke several air holes around the bottle top.

3 Add a handful of rocks to the bottle so the bottom is covered.

4 Add a layer of sand to the bottle. The sand should just about cover the rocks.

5 Add a layer of dirt to the bottle. The dirt should be about 2 inches (5 cm) deep.

Continued on the next page.

6 Add a few worms and some worm food to the dirt.

7 Repeat steps 4 through 6 until the top layer is 1 to 2 inches (2.5 to 5 cm) from the top edge of the bottle.

8 Add just enough water to the bottle to get the dirt wet.

9 Place the bottle top back onto the bottle bottom and tape it in place. Make sure not to cover up the air holes.

Grossed Out!

As worms move through soil, they loosen it. This makes it easier for air and water to enter the soil. Worms also eat dead plants and other matter in soil. Then, worm droppings **fertilize** the soil!

10 Decorate a piece of construction paper.

11 Wrap the paper around the bottle to form a tube. Tape the **seam**.

12 Keep your worms in a cool, dark place with the bottle cap off. Every few days, add more water and worm food to the bottle. Remove the construction paper to see how busy your worms have been!

11

SLITHERING
RATTLESNAKE

This cool cup-snake slithers and shakes just like a real rattlesnake.

MATERIALS

- colored paper cups
- duct tape
- craft knife
- brass fasteners
- scissors
- toilet paper tube
- popcorn kernels
- stapler
- googly eyes
- craft glue
- chenille stem

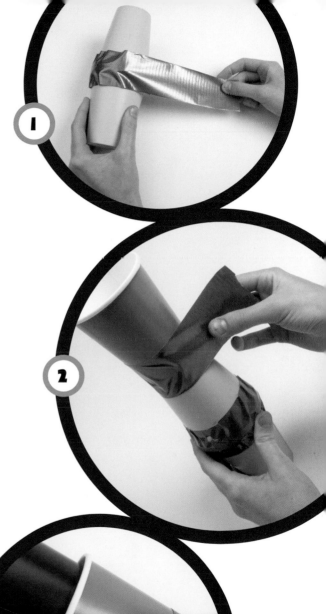

1 Stack two cups with their openings facing each other. Tape the cups along the **seam**. This is the snake's head.

2 Stack a third cup onto the first two so the bottoms face each other. Tape the cup in place.

3 Lay the cups on their sides. Slide the bottom of another cup about 1 inch (2.5 cm) into the open end of the third cup.

4 Have an adult help poke a hole through the sides of both cups. The hole should be about ½ inch (1.2 cm) from the top edge of the outside cup. Push a brass fastener through both holes and secure it.

Continued on the next page.

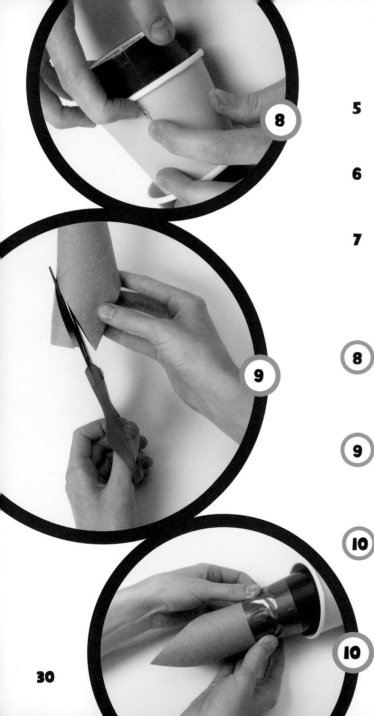

5   Repeat step 4 on the other side of the cups.

6   Repeat steps 4 and 5 as you add at least six more cups to the snake's body.

7   Trim about 2 inches (5 cm) off the top of a new cup. Then slide the trimmed cup into the last cup of the snake's body. The bottom of the trimmed cup should face out.

8   Repeat step 4 to secure the last cup with a brass fastener, but switch the direction of the fastener so the round head is inside the cup.

9   Cut the toilet paper tube to about 4 inches (10 cm) long. Flatten one end of the tube and cut it to make a point.

10   Tape the uncut end of the tube to the bottom of the final cup.

11 Pour a handful of popcorn kernels into the tube.

12 Staple the pointed end of the tube closed. Cover the tube with duct tape. This piece represents the rattlesnake's rattle!

13 Decorate your snake's face with googly eyes and a chenille stem tongue.

Grossed Out!

Rattlesnakes get their name from the rattle at the tip of their tails. This rattle is made of keratin, the same material your fingernails are made of. The buzzing sound of the rattle warns predators to stay away.

31

GLOSSARY

axle – a bar that connects two wheels.

digestive – relating to digestion. Digestion is the process of breaking down food so the body can use it.

disease – a sickness.

disgust – a strong feeling of dislike toward something unpleasant or offensive. Something that gives the feeling of disgust is described as disgusting.

ecosystem – a group of plants and animals that live together in nature and depend on each other to survive.

edible – safe to eat.

fascinate – to interest or charm.

fertilize – to add something to soil to make plants grow better.

infection – a sickness caused by the presence of bacteria or other germs.

resilient – able to become strong or healthy again after something bad happens.

scurry – to walk or run using short, quick steps.

seam – the line where two edges meet.